GOTTA HAVE GOD

A Devotional for Boys Ages 4–7

Illustrated by
Olga & Aleksey Ivanov

HENDRICKSON
PUBLISHERS

R🌹SE
KiDZ

www.hendricksonrose.com

www.hendricksonrose.com

Gotta Have God A Devotional for Boys Ages 4-7
©2016 Rose Publishing, All rights reserved.

Contributors: Georgia Varozza and Jean Christen

Rose Kidz® is an imprint of
Rose Publishing, LLC
P.O. Box 3473
Peabody, Massachusetts 01961-3473 USA
www.hendricksonrose.com

Cover and interior design by Mary pat Pino
Illustrated by Olga and Aleksey Ivanov

ISBN: 978-1-584111-74-0
RoseKidz® reorder number (Product Code) L46970
Juvenile Nonfiction/Religious/Christian/Devotional & Prayer

Printed in South Korea   02   12.2017.APC

"To all children of God"

O.&A. I.

Be kind to one another. Ephesians 4:32

Daddy called, "Boys, let's go to the hardware store. Then we will get ice cream."

Ben clapped his hands. "Ice cream!" His big brother Josh jumped up. "The hardware store!"

Daddy loved to surprise his boys. At the store, Ben sat in the cart. Josh walked beside, while Daddy pushed. There was so much to see! Daddy bought things he needed, and then they went to the ice cream store, where Daddy got three ice cream cones. They walked with their cones to sit under a big tree to eat them.

Suddenly, Ben's ice cream fell right off the cone. Oh, NO! But there it was, on the ground, all dirty. Ben started to cry. Josh felt sad for Ben. He remembered times when his ice cream had fallen to the ground.

"Don't cry," said Josh. "Here. Have a bite of my ice cream." Ben smiled and took a bite. YUM!

Daddy said, "Thank you for being kind, Josh. That makes God happy. It makes me happy, too! In fact, you can give your cone to Ben. Because I will give my cone to YOU. We can all be kind!"

Talk About It

Who was sad? Who was kind?

How do you feel when someone is kind to you?

What are two ways you can be kind to someone in your family?

Try This!

Use your finger to trace the path from the ice cream store to the big tree. Point to some kind people there!

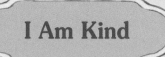

Prayer

God, thank You for being
kind to us. Please help us to be
kind. We know it makes You happy.
It makes us happy, too!
Amen.

Day 2: I Can Obey

Children, obey your parents in the Lord, for this is right.

Ephesians 6:1

It was nearly time for Logan's birthday party, and Michael was all ready to go!

"Can I play outside until we leave?" Michael asked.

"No," Mom said. "Please stay indoors. You are all clean for the party. It's muddy outside."

But Michael still wanted to play outside with his dog, Spot! So when Michael's mother went to get ready, he went out to the porch. Then he stood on the sidewalk and picked up Spot's ball.

Spot came running! He wanted to play! UH-OH! Spot jumped up on Michael, and pushed him into a muddy puddle! Now Michael was dirty and wet. He heard his mother calling.

"Michael? Where are you?" Mom came out onto the porch. "I can see you did not obey me," she said. "Now you have to take another bath. You will be late for Logan's party."

Michael sat in the tub, sad and mad. But he knew he did not obey his mom. If he had obeyed, they would be at Logan's party now.

Michael sighed. He said, "God, I am sorry. Please help me to obey next time." Now he felt clean on the inside AND the outside. He jumped out, dried off, and put on clean clothes. Ready again!

Talk About It!

What happened when Michael did not obey?

How did he feel? What did he miss?

What are times you obey your parents?

How do you feel when you obey your mom or dad?

Try This!

When have you gotten muddy? There is a lot of mud in this picture.
But there is something else. Can you see what it is?

Prayer

Dear Jesus, thank You for
loving me, even when I mess up.
Please help me obey my mom and dad.
Amen.

Day 3: I Am Thankful

Give thanks to the Lord, for he is good. Psalm 136:1

Ethan opened his eyes and sat up. Then he remembered—TODAY is ZOO DAY! He jumped out of bed and found his elephant shirt. He put on his pants and shoes, then jumped, bump, bump, bump, down the stairs.

"Good morning, Ethan!" Daddy said. "I think you're ready for our adventure!"

"YES!" said Ethan. Let's GO!" Daddy laughed.

"Let's eat first," Mommy said. "That will give us lots of energy for our time at the zoo."

Ethan said, "Daddy, can I pray before we eat?" They held hands and closed their eyes.

"Dear God," Ethan prayed, "thank You for the animals You made. Thank You for Mommy and Daddy. Thank You that I get to go to the zoo. Thank You for this food. You are good! Amen."

Daddy said, "Amen. You're right, Ethan. God is good!"

Mommy said, "And we are thankful!"

Talk About It!

Name your favorite animal. Who made that animal?

What is a food you like to eat? Who gives us food?

Name a person who loves you. Who made that person?

Try This!

Touch each petal of the flower. With each touch, name something that makes you glad. Say, "Thank you, God!" for each thing you name.

Prayer

Dear Jesus, thank You for
giving me people who love me.
Thank You for happy times.
Help me to be thankful
ALL the time!
Amen.

Day 4: I Can Trust God

Do not fear, for I am with you. Isaiah 41:10

The sky was dark and full of clouds. Connor shivered. He was chilly—and scared.

"The storm's really picking up," Dad said. "I'm glad we're inside, safe and warm. I just hope the electricity doesn't go out."

But no sooner had Dad said that then POOF, the lights went out! Connor was more scared.

"We will light some candles," said Mom. When she lit the candles, they made a warm glow.

But when Connor looked at the wall, the shadows were moving and changing!

"Daddy!" said Connor. "The shadows are moving. They look like monsters!"

Dad hugged Connor. "You don't need be afraid," Dad said. "The air is moving in the room. That moving air makes the candles flicker. And when the candle flames flicker and move, the shadows move, too. They are only shadows. And remember, God is with us."

16

Connor grabbed his daddy a little tighter. "Let's ask God to help us not be afraid." So Dad prayed, and Connor felt better.

Then Dad said, "I have an idea. Let's get our blankets and pillows. We'll camp together in the living room!"

Soon, Connor was snuggled down in his blankets and pillows. The candle shadows looked funny, but not scary. He was warm and cozy. God was with him. Dad and Mom were with him. He smiled—and fell asleep!

17

Talk About It!

Have you ever lost the lights at your house? What happened?

What is something scary to you?

What is something you can do when you are scared?

Who is always with us? Who will help us?

Try This!

When it is dark, try this with your family. Shine a flashlight at the wall. Put your hands in front of the light to make fun shapes. Can you make these shapes?

Prayer

Jesus, thank You that
You are with me always,
even when I am scared.
Amen.

Day 5: I Can Be Brave

Trust in the LORD with all your heart. Proverbs 3:5

"Come on, Jacob. You can do it!" Daddy said.

Jacob stood at the edge of the swimming pool. Daddy wanted him to jump to him into the deep end of the pool.

"I'm scared, Daddy," cried Jacob. "What if I go under the water and don't come up?"

"I'll catch you," said Daddy. "You can trust me! Remember when I helped you learn to ride your bike?"

Jacob nodded. He remembered. He'd been scared then too, but Daddy had helped him. He taught Jacob how to keep his balance. And now he wasn't scared of riding his bike. He loved to ride it everywhere!

Jacob thought. His dad was right there to catch him. He could be brave!

"Okay, Daddy, I'm ready. One, two, three . . . !"

He jumped SPLASH! and his dad caught him even before his head got wet!

"Jacob," said Daddy, "You did it! You were brave!"

Jacob said, "I knew you would help me."

Daddy said, "That's how it is with God, too. We can trust Him to help us be brave."

"God is here? Even in the pool?" Jacob asked.

"Even in the pool!" said Daddy.

21

Talk About It!

What do you like to do in the water?

Who helps kids learn to swim?

Who can help us to be brave?

What can we do when we don't feel brave?

Try This!

This boy is on an adventure. He's asking God to help him be brave.

How many hills can you count? How many pointy trees? How many round bushes?

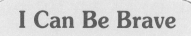

I Can Be Brave

Prayer

Thank You, God, that I can trust You to help me. Please remind me to ask for your help when I don't feel brave.
Amen.

Day 6: I Can Rejoice

Rejoice in the Lord always. I will say it again: Rejoice! Philippians 4:4 (NIV)

Daddy read aloud from his Bible, "Rejoice in the Lord always. I will say it again: Rejoice!"

"What does 'rejoice' mean?" asked Max.

"That's a great question," said Daddy. "When we rejoice, we show we are joyful or happy. There will be times when we are sad. But even in sad times, we can rejoice. That's why it says to rejoice always. We can always trust God to bring something good, even out of a sad time."

"When I was your age my family moved. I had to leave my friends and switch schools. I was very sad. But on the first day, I met a new friend, Ray. We have been best friends ever since."

"What I thought would be a terrible day, turned out to the best day ever."

Max said, "Today was like that! My friend Ryan was acting mean. So I played with Logan instead. We had a good time. He even invited me to his birthday party this Saturday!"

Daddy smiled. "Wow! God took good care of you. Let's rejoice and thank Him for turning what started as a sad thing into a glad thing!"

Talk About It!

When Ryan was acting mean, what did Max do? What happened?

Why can we rejoice, even when things seem bad?

Ask a parent, "Tell me about a time when God surprised you with His goodness." Listen to the story. Then rejoice and thank God for that time!

Try This!

What are some ways to rejoice? You could sing a song of praise to God or play an instrument. You could write a poem or draw a picture. You could jump! Choose one to do—and rejoice while you do it!

Prayer

Dear Jesus, thank You for loving me. Thank You that when I have a hard time, I can trust You to bring good things out of sad things. Help me to always rejoice! Amen.

Day 7: I Can Accept Others

Accept one another, then, just as Christ accepted you, in order to bring praise to God. Romans 15:7 (NIV)

Asher walked into the kitchen. His mom was making tea. He said, "There was a new boy at church today. He comes from a different country. When he talks, I can't always understand him. Our teacher talked to us about being kind today. So I tried to talk to him. But it was hard."

Mommy said, "Come have a cup of tea with me!" Asher and his mom sat down together.

"When you come from a different country, it's hard work to learn a new language. That could be why you don't understand his words. But if you think about it, everyone is different. You have brown hair and blue eyes. But your baby brother has blond hair and green eyes. You're big and he's small. But you both enjoy playing with trucks and building blocks. You have things in common."

Mommy continued, "Your friend Kai has black hair and brown eyes. His family came from Japan. God made each of us different. But you both enjoy playing together."

"I'll ask the new boy to play with me next week," said Asher. "If we play together, he won't seem so different."

Mommy gave Asher a big hug. "I think you're right, son. God loves the world and everyone in it. We should too."

Talk About It!

Think of one of your friends. What are two ways God made you different from that friend?

What are some things you are good at?

What are ways you can show kindness to a kid you don't know?

Try This!

Look at all the kids on this page! Find at least five ways they are all alike. Then find ways each one is different from the kid next to him or her.

31

Prayer

Dear Jesus, thank You for new friends and for old friends. Please help me to accept others the way You love and accept me! Amen.